Simple Machines

Cody Crane

Content Consultant

Elizabeth Case DeSantis, M.A. Elementary Education
Julia A. Stark Elementary School, Stamford, Connecticut

Reading Consultant

Jeanne M. Clidas, Ph.D.
Reading Specialist

Children's Press®
An Imprint of Scholastic Inc.

Library of Congress Cataloging-in-Publication Data
Names: Crane, Cody, author.
Title: Simple machines/by Cody Crane.
Other titles: Rookie read-about science.
Description: New York, NY USA: Children's Press,
an imprint of Scholastic Inc., 2019. | Series: Rookie read-about
science | Includes index.
Identifiers: LCCN 2018027648| ISBN 9780531134061 (library
binding) | ISBN 9780531138007 (pbk.)
Subjects: LCSH: Simple machines--Juvenile literature.
Classification: LCC TJ147 .C73 2019 | DDC 621.8--dc23

Produced by Spooky Cheetah Press
Design: Kimberly Shake
Digital Imaging: Bianca Alexis
Creative Direction: Judith E. Christ for Scholastic Inc.
© 2019 by Scholastic Inc. All rights reserved.

Published in 2019 by Children's Press, an imprint of
Scholastic Inc.

Printed in Heshan, China 62

1 2 3 4 5 6 7 8 9 10 R 28 27 26 25 24 23 22 21 20 19

Scholastic Inc., 557 Broadway, New York,
NY 10012

Photos ©: cover foreground: abadonian/iStockphoto;
cover background: tcharts/Shutterstock; back cover:
RichVantage/Getty Images; 2-3: Zero Creatives/Getty
Images; 5: guvendemir/iStockphoto; 7: Valueline/Getty
Images; 9 top right: viti/iStockphoto; 9 center left: David
Leahy/Getty Images; 9 center right: Photo Researchers/
Getty Images; 9 bottom left: GIPhotoStock/Science Source;
9 bottom right: Phil Degginger/Science Source; 9 top left:
RichVantage/Getty Images; 10: © johnlund.com; 13: Mieke
Dalle/Getty Images; 15: Vitalliy/Shutterstock; 17: Gary
Rhijnsburger/Masterfile; 19: MECKY/Getty Images; 20-21
background: Benjamin Egerland/EyeEm/Getty Images;
20 tortoise: Smileus/Shutterstock; 21 dog: master1305/
iStockphoto; 22: Thinkstock Images/Getty Images; 25: EMS-
FORSTER-PRODUCTIONS/Getty Images; 27: Charlottep68/
Dreamstime; 28-29 all other images: Jennifer A. Uihlein;
29 marshmallow: subjug/iStockphoto; 30 top: Mieke Dalle/
Getty Images; 30 center: Vitalliy/Shutterstock; 30 bottom
seesaw: Benjamin Egerland/EyeEm/Getty Images; 30 bottom
dog: master1305/iStockphoto; 30 bottom tortoise: Smileus/
Shutterstock; 31 top: guvendemir/iStockphoto; 31 center:
Gary Rhijnsburger/Masterfile; 31 bottom: Thinkstock Images/
Getty Images; 32: John Lund/Getty Images.

Table of Contents

Chapter 1

Ready to Work

Machines make work easier. Some machines have lots of moving parts. They help people do tough jobs.

5

Machines can have few or no moving parts, too. These simple machines do simple jobs.

How do wheels make it easier to pull this wagon?

There are six types
of simple machines.

Have
you ever
used any of
these simple
machines?

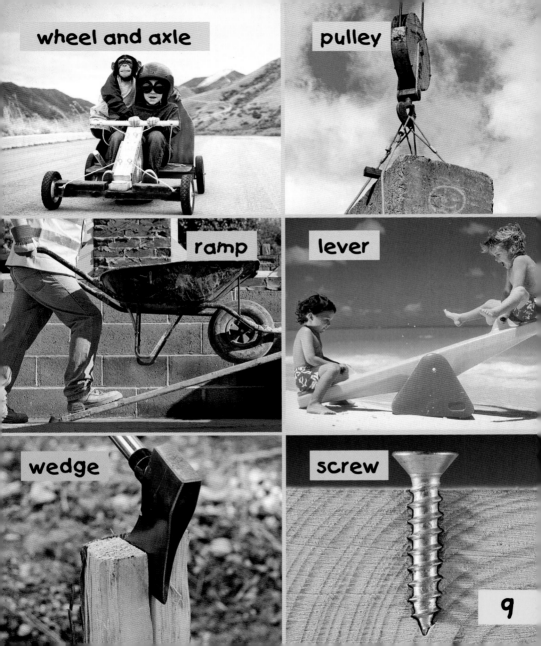

wheel and axle

pulley

ramp

lever

wedge

screw

9

Chapter 2

On a Roll

Wheels help things roll. Skateboards and bikes have wheels. Wheels make them go.

How does the shape of the wheels help the bike roll?

A wheel could not turn without an **axle**. An axle is a pole fixed to the center of a wheel.

How many wheels and axles does this skateboard have?

13

An axle keeps a wheel **balanced** as it turns.

Where is the axle on the Ferris wheel?

15

Chapter 3

Going Up

A **pulley** helps lift things. It is made up of a rope wrapped around a wheel.

Does the pulley make it easier or harder to lift the bucket?

members only!

wheel

rope

keep out

17

A ramp is also a useful tool to lift things. Pushing an object up a ramp is easier than lifting it straight up.

Could this worker move these large boxes without the ramp?

19

A **lever** is anything that rests on a point. Pushing down on one end of the lever lifts the other side. You can use a lever to move or lift something heavy.

How could you make the dog's side go down?

Why is the tortoise's side of the seesaw on the ground?

Chapter 4

Cut It Out

A **wedge** helps split things in two. The top of this tool is thick. The other end is thin. The shape helps push things apart. An ax is a wedge used to cut wood.

Why does an ax have a handle?

A screw turns. It cuts into a piece of wood as it twirls around. A screw is used to hold things together.

Do you know the name of the tool that is used to turn a screw?

Simple machines roll, lift, and cut. They help us do lots of everyday jobs. Together, these tools make up the parts of even bigger, hardworking machines.

Can you name a simple machine that is part of this monster truck?

Build a Catapult

Use a simple machine to hurl things.

Remember to ask an adult for help with this activity.

1. Stack six craft sticks. Wrap a rubber band around each end of the stack.

2. Set the stack between two craft sticks and wrap a rubber band around one end of the two sticks.

3. Wrap another rubber band where the two sticks cross the stack.

4. Glue a bottle cap to the top craft stick at the unbanded end. Place a pom-pom or marshmallow in the cap. Push down. Let it go.

What Happened?

A catapult is really a lever. The top stick rests on a point. When you let go of the cap, it springs back. That flings your object into the air.

axle (**ak**-suhl): a rod in the center of a wheel, around which the wheel turns

- *A wheel could not turn without an* **axle**.

balanced (bal-**uhn**-st): having the ability to stay stable and upright

- *A Ferris wheel has to stay* **balanced**.

lever (**leh**-var): a bar resting on a pivot used to lift an object on one end by pushing down on the other

- *A seesaw is a type of* **lever**.

machines (muh-**sheenz**): equipment whose different pieces work together to do a job

- **Machines** *make work easier.*

---

pulley (**pul**-lee): a wheel with a grooved rim around which a rope or chain can run

- *A* **pulley** *helps lift things.*

---

wedge (**wej**): something that is thin and pointed at one end and thick at the other and is used to push things apart

- *An ax is a type of* **wedge**.

Index

Facts for Now

Visit this Scholastic website for more information on Simple Machines, and to download the Reader's Guide for this series:
http://www.factsfornow. scholastic.com
Enter the keywords **Simple Machines**

About the Author

Cody Crane is an award-winning children's science writer. She lives in Texas with her husband and son.